YOU'RE IN BUSINESS!

GET A JOB

HELPING OTHERS

Ryan Jacobson

Illustrations by Jon Cannell

Lerner Publications • Minneapolis

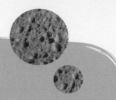

For Jonah and Lucas. May you always be
willing to lend a helping hand. —R.J.

For Mrs. Bell, my kindergarten teacher who
loved teaching and was an inspiration to
all of us. —J.C.

Lerner Publications Company
A division of Lerner Publishing Group, Inc.
241 First Avenue North
Minneapolis, MN 55401 USA

For reading levels and more information, look up this title
at www.lernerbooks.com.

Library of Congress Cataloging-in-Publication Data

Jacobson, Ryan.
    Get a job helping others / Ryan Jacobson.
        p.   cm. — (You're in business!)
    Includes index.
    ISBN 978-1-4677-3836-1 (lib. bdg. : alk. paper)
    ISBN 978-1-4677-4756-1 (EB pdf)
        1. Moneymaking projects for children—Juvenile
    literature. 2. Business—Juvenile literature.
        3. Entrepreneurship—Juvenile literature. I. Title.
    HF5392.J33 2015
    331.702—dc23   2013039047

Manufactured in the United States of America
2 - BP - 3/15/15

TABLE OF CONTENTS

Introduction: You Provide the Service. They Provide the Cash. . . . 4

Lawn Mowing . . . 6

Yard Services . . . 10

Babysitting . . . 13

Dog Walking . . . 17

Car Washing . . . 20

Garage Organizing . . . 24

Tutoring . . . 28

Teaching Social Media . . . 32

Parting Words . . . 35

Now What? . . . 36

Glossary . . . 37

Further Information . . . 38

Index . . . 39

YOU PROVIDE THE SERVICE.

THEY PROVIDE THE CASH.

When was the last time you did someone a favor? Maybe a friend needed help understanding a math assignment. Or perhaps your neighbor's car was long overdue for a good scrub. If you look around your neighborhood, you'll find plenty of ways to help out.

Nothing beats the satisfaction of helping others. But sometimes that warm, fuzzy feeling can go hand in hand with some cold, hard cash. If you offer a useful service, you can turn your good deeds into a good business. From mowing your neighbors' yards to babysitting for local families, job opportunities are everywhere.

With the right attitude and strategy, you can make hundreds of dollars! And you can offer a helping hand to people in your community while you're at it.

You're never too young to help others. And that means you're not too young to start earning money.

LAWN MOWING

When it comes to jobs, there's usually a trade-off: the harder you work, the more money you make. That's definitely true for lawn mowing. It takes a lot of effort, but it pays very well.

If you like to sweat, if you enjoy being outside, and if you don't mind working alone, lawn mowing might be the job for you. But before you launch your new business, you're going to need a few things. A mower, a gas can (with gasoline), a trimmer, a schedule book, and business cards will be enough to get you started.

If your home has a yard, your family might already own this stuff. If so, get permission to use the equipment. If not, you'll need to invest a few hundred dollars to buy it. Talk to a parent or a guardian. See if you can make a plan for borrowing money from him or her. Or perhaps you can

borrow it from another relative. Be sure to make a plan for paying the money back. Also, remember to set aside cash to buy gasoline. From time to time, your mower will need maintenance, such as oil changes and blade sharpening. With your family, decide how much money you'll pitch in to cover these costs.

Next, you'll need practice, which means mowing some lawns for free. Of course, your family will probably be thrilled to let you mow your own yard, if you have one. But you'll want to practice on other yards too. Ask neighbors or family friends if you can mow for them. Volunteer to mow at local nonprofit businesses. It's good experience, but that's not all. The people you mow for might turn into paying customers. And you may be able to use them as references when you're searching for more clients.

Working Wisdom: Business Cards

Nothing says "professional" like your own business card. Your cards should look nice, but they don't need to be fancy. You can pay to get them professionally printed. Or you can make them yourself. To create your own cards, use thick, high-quality paper such as card stock. On a computer, type the information that should go on the card: your name, the service you provide, and your phone number or e-mail address. Make a table or spreadsheet with cells that match the size you want your cards to be. Copy your information into each cell. Then print the spreadsheet on the card stock. Cut up the card stock into small rectangular pieces, with a copy of your information on each piece.

With enough practice, you're ready to start making money. Grab your schedule book and your business cards. Then start knocking on doors. You're a door-to-door salesperson, and you're selling your lawn mowing services.

Stay close to home, at least at first. (When it's time to mow, you won't want to drag your equipment all the way across town.) Skip places with yards that are too big to handle. And if you come to a home with freshly mowed grass, you might want to wait and knock on that door another day.

When you do knock, be professional and polite. Know what you're going to say when someone answers the door. A pitch like this will work: "Hi, I'm Joe from down the street. I've been mowing yards for the Johnsons, the Rodriguezes, and the volunteer fire department. I wonder if you might be interested in hiring me to mow your lawn."

More often than not, the answer will be "No, thanks." But leave your business card. Some people might change their minds, or they might need you to mow while they're away on vacation.

Once in a while, you might get a maybe. In that case, you can offer to trim around the edges of their home for free, just to show them that you know what you're doing. Leave a business card, and if they're still undecided, offer to follow up with them in a few days. (Then put a reminder in your schedule book to do so.)

When you get a yes, it's time to figure out the details. Agree on a plan with your clients: "I'd like to mow on Saturdays from three to four p.m., and I'll plan on mowing your yard every week. Does that work for you?" Note the plan in your schedule book. Give your clients a business card, and get their contact information. Remember to discuss when you'll get paid too. It will probably be as soon as you finish the work. But if your clients aren't home, you might need to stop by at a different time.

Speaking of payment, you're probably wondering how much to charge. Rates vary depending on what's typical for your area and how much time the job will take. The size of the yard and the number of objects to trim around (such as trees and swing sets) play a part in the amount of work you'll be doing, so consider those factors when setting your rates.

The amount you earn per job matters less than the effort and time you put into making your business successful. With hard work and good customer service, you're sure to turn a profit sooner or later.

YARD SERVICES

Maybe you like the idea of working outside, but mowing lawns isn't right for you. Or perhaps you do want to mow, and you'd like to offer other services too. Either way, there's another option: you can go into business providing yard services.

If there's work to be done in someone's yard, it can be done by you. This can mean anything from raking a yard to shoveling snow. Weeding, picking up sticks, cleaning up after pets, and tending a garden are other possibilities. Of course, the type of work available depends on where you live. There won't be a lot of snow in southern states. And it might be hard to find raking jobs in urban areas or

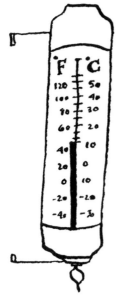

desert climates. Still, if you think creatively, you can usually get some work. For instance, in an urban area, you may be able to help with a rooftop garden or a community garden.

Compared to lawn mowing, the startup costs for yard services are low. You'll need only a few inexpensive supplies, such as trash bags to put leaves in. Your customers will likely have rakes and shovels that you can use. But you'll seem more professional if you bring your own.

As with mowing lawns, your first step is to practice by volunteering. Neighbors, family friends, and local nonprofits will appreciate your help. Rake as many lawns, pull as many weeds, and shovel as many driveways as you can. Do it until you understand the work and until you can tell how long any given job will take.

When you're ready to find paying clients, the best approach is to go door-to-door. Choose your timing carefully. The day after the year's first snowfall is a great time to scope out sidewalks and driveways that haven't been shoveled—and pinpoint potential clients. But you also don't have to wait until people are desperate for help. Look for homes with trees in or near their yards. Stop by in late summer and ask the owners if they could use your raking services in a few months.

You might provide some yard services on an "on call" basis. This means that you have work to do, but you're not sure when you'll need to do it. If you're on call, clients

contact you when they need you. For jobs such as raking leaves or picking up fallen tree branches, your customers will call only when there's enough work to be done.

If your services include shoveling snow, you might be on call— even though your clients never contact you. That's because you'll already know when there's work to do. Customers should be able to count on you to shovel after every snowfall.

When you find paying customers, discuss these options with them. Make sure you and your clients agree on how much you'll get paid, how often you'll work, and whether you'll be on call. Tell them about the other services you offer too. Hand out business cards, and invite them to contact you as needed.

Working Wisdom: Door-Knocking

Going door-to-door can drum up a lot of clients for your business. When you hit the pavement, dress nicely—nothing dirty or ripped. Let a parent or guardian know where you're going and how long you plan to be gone. (He or she might even want to come with you.) If you head out on your own, bring a cell phone.

Choose a day and time when people are likely to be home, such as Saturday afternoon. Keep in mind that people often don't come to the door during mealtimes. Some homes have No Soliciting signs posted. These might not apply to you—since you're offering a service, not just asking for money—but be prepared for a brush-off if you decide to knock at these places.

If anyone is rude to you, politely say, "Sorry to have bothered you," and move on. When you do get a chance to make a pitch, don't talk for more than a couple of minutes. And always thank people for their time.

BABYSITTING

Babysitting is a popular first job—and for good reason. It sounds like a fun way to make money, and it certainly can be fun. But it's not as simple as getting paid to play with kids. Working as a babysitter is a very big responsibility.

To be a good babysitter, you should enjoy children. But the job also requires a lot of patience and energy. And it takes someone who doesn't mind being in charge. If that sounds like you, then babysitting might be right up your alley.

The most important steps to becoming a good babysitter happen before you ever go to work. Watching children is far from predictable, so you need to be prepared. What will you do if a child pees on the floor? What if the kids break a window? How will you handle a tantrum? A scraped knee? Or—worst of all—what if there's an emergency?

To handle these challenges, you'll need some training. Start by taking courses on first aid, basic child care, and child safety.

Classes are sometimes available through community education, community centers, hospitals, or even online. The more training you get, the more confidence you'll have. Plus, with all that training, you'll be a babysitter who's in demand. Parents will want to hire you.

Experience is just as valuable as training. You can learn a lot by volunteering at a local day care or even at a children's hospital. You can co-teach a class at a house of worship. Or you can help supervise young kids at a community center. And offer to watch the children of your relatives, family friends, and neighbors. They might pay you for your time, but it's best if you're willing to do it for free. The volunteer time you put in early should get you some good references. That'll lead to more paid opportunities later on. (Even after you become a paid babysitter, keep volunteering wherever you can. Not only is it a nice thing to do—it will also appeal to potential clients.)

Before you start charging, you've got some big decisions to make. First, what types of situations are you comfortable with? Unless you're a champion diaper-changer and bottle-feeder, you probably shouldn't watch children younger than two. But what about kids who are only a couple of years younger

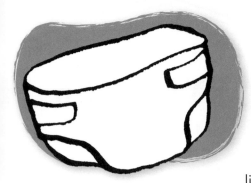

than you? If you're not confident they'll respect your authority, you may not be the right sitter for them. Does spending a few hours with five rowdy kids sound like a nightmare? Then skip those gigs.

Do you feel capable of watching children with special needs? Are you afraid of big dogs? Allergic to cats? You should carefully consider each job offer and decide if it's right for you. If something about a situation makes you uneasy, it's okay to say, "No thanks."

When you do land a job, the other thing you'll have to decide is how much to charge. It might feel awkward to discuss this with your clients, but if you don't, be prepared to get underpaid. So have set rates. That way, you can tell the parents what you expect to be paid before you accept the job. Usually it's a few dollars per child per hour. (And you can charge extra for children who are especially challenging.) Ask other babysitters what they charge, and ask a few trusted adults what they typically pay. That should give you an idea of the going rate in your area.

Your rate doesn't have to be set in stone, either. If a family wants your services but can't afford to pay what you charge, be willing to negotiate. Let them make you an offer of what they can pay. If it's too low to be worth your time, you can say no. But you should at least consider lowering your price for a family in need.

To spread the word about your new business, let family, friends, and

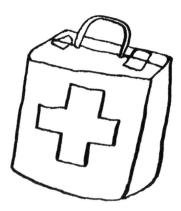

neighbors know that you're looking for work. Someone will give you a chance—especially after all the training and volunteering you've done. From there, the best way to grow your business is to be awesome! If you're the world's best babysitter, parents are going to tell other parents about you.

And how are you going to be the world's best babysitter? By being prepared.

Your most important job is to keep the kids safe. Ask the parents for emergency contact information. Know where to find first-aid supplies and fire extinguishers. Find out if the kids have allergies or food restrictions.

You also need to maintain control and enforce the family rules. Learn these rules up front. When is bedtime? What activities, TV channels, or snacks are off-limits? What are the consequences for bad behavior?

Keep safety and discipline at the front of your mind. Then give the kids a fun and educational time. Plan activities in advance. Get the parents' permission to go to the park, have a scavenger hunt, or paint pictures. Do something special every time you babysit. Bring new activities and ideas on each visit.

If the kids cheer when they hear you're coming and if the parents know you're keeping the kids safe and in control, you'll get a lot of work. Better yet, you'll probably come to find that the affection of a child is far more valuable than a paycheck.

DOG WALKING

Nearly 57 million households in the United States have dogs, and chances are some of them are near you. Many dog owners would be happy to pay a dog walker. So if you love animals, this might be a good chance to carve out your own business.

Dog walking is usually more than just walking a dog. Yes, you'll be expected to walk the dog at least once or twice a day. (Some dog walkers walk more than one dog at a time.) But you might also be expected to play with the dog, feed the dog, and even bathe the dog.

Be sure to give dog walking a try before you go into business. Make sure it's a job that you enjoy doing and are able to handle. To get some experience, volunteer at a local animal shelter or at a veterinarian's office. You can also help care for the pets of family, friends, and neighbors.

The next step is to advertise your services. Start with a door-to-door approach. Go around the neighborhood to all the local dog owners. Introduce yourself, and let them know about your services.

Working Wisdom: Getting the Word Out

When you go into business, let others advertise for you. Ask your friends and relatives to tell *their* friends and relatives about your business. You could even offer a referral bonus. For instance, you could pay ten dollars to anyone who helps you get a new client.

(Be sure to mention the volunteer work you do. It should impress them.) Whether they say yes, no, or maybe, leave a business card behind, so they can call you if they need you.

Since you're just starting, keep your rates low. For instance, if you charge five dollars and spend only twenty minutes walking a dog, that still adds up to fifteen dollars per hour of work—a pretty good wage. As your business grows and as you add more and more clients, you can always raise your rates. (But if you start losing too many clients, you've raised your rates too high!)

Once you're hired, plan your routes in advance. Stay away from busy roads, and avoid walking past homes with loud or aggressive animals. Keep each client's pet safe and happy. Find out from the owner if the dog has any specific fears, dislikes, or quirks that you need to watch out for. If Rusty is terrified of water, be

prepared to guide him past a
sprinkler spraying the sidewalk
or puddles from last night's
rainstorm. If Lulu won't do her
business until she's paced back
and forth for several minutes, get used to
waiting while she does her routine. Always bring bags to
clean up the dog's poop. The pet is likely to leave a mess somewhere.
It's your job to pick it up and dispose of it.

As you build up your client list, you might want to save space on
your business cards. A good dog walker can often turn into a first-rate
pet sitter.

A pet sitter takes care of people's pets when the owners are out of
town. That means playing with the pets, feeding them, and cleaning
up their messes. You'll probably visit an owner's home several times
a day at specific times. If you take good care of the pets, leave the
home the way you found it, and don't lose the owner's spare keys,
you'll have a lock on your new side business.

Many dog owners consider their pets
to be their "children." The dogs are part
of the family. Treat the dogs with love
and respect, and the pet owners will be
pleased with your work.

CAR WASHING

If you're a car fanatic, there's a great job that can get you up close to all sorts of vehicles. Or if you simply enjoy cleaning, the same job might be for you. Washing cars can be a casual, fun, and simple way to earn money.

You'd better not mind getting a little wet and dirty. You also need to be thorough, with good attention to detail. If you're fast enough, you can do the job alone. But it might be more fun to share the work (and the profits) with one or more reliable, hardworking friends.

Unlike a lot of other jobs, this one doesn't demand a set schedule. Most clients won't want their cars washed every week. So the key to a successful car-washing business is having plenty of customers.

If other car washes are nearby, ask yourself how you're going to be different—better—than they are. You're already a step ahead of self-service car washes because you're offering to do the work for your clients. You'll also get some notice if you do a better job than the competition and if your rates are low. That shouldn't be a problem,

CAR WASH

because this business costs very little to operate. You only need to pay for a few buckets, some sponges, car washing soap (which is sold by the gallon and will last a long time), some towels—and maybe part of a water bill.

Once you've got your supplies, work on mastering the art of car washing. Your goal should be to clean the outside of a car in less than fifteen minutes. Start with the top and work your way down. Apply soap to one section of the car at a time. Then rinse that section before moving on, so that the soap doesn't dry and stain the car. Save the wheels for last. These are the dirtiest parts of the car, so you may want to keep a special sponge for them. When you're done, dry the car with fresh towels.

To practice your car-washing skills, scrub relatives' vehicles from top to bottom. You can also visit local car dealerships. Car dealers work hard to keep their cars clean, and they might be willing to show you a few tricks.

Look for places to volunteer. If anyone in town is doing a car-wash fund-raiser, see if you can help. And who else has a vehicle that you can clean? Not only will the practice make you better at your job—you'll develop a good reputation in your community. That's going to help your business.

Working Wisdom: Flyers

When it comes to advertising, flyers are like jumbo business cards. They have room for all your basic information, plus extra space for specifics about your skills and availability. They can also promote a specific event or one-time service you're offering. You can make flyers by hand or design them on a computer. The more colorful, the better. Pictures or background designs can add flair too. Just don't let the page get too cluttered. Make sure the information is still easy to read.

Next, you'll need to find a location for your work—someplace that gets a lot of traffic. The corner of a shopping center parking lot is ideal, but you'll have to get permission to be there. Some places might let you do it once or twice, but it could be tough to find a permanent location.

If so, you can become a traveling car wash. Offer to go to your clients' homes and clean their cars right in their driveways. That's added convenience for your customers. (And in that case, you can try a door-to-door approach to getting business.)

Consider launching your new venture with a day of free car washes. Find a good place to set up. Then, a week or two before the big day, begin advertising. Hang up flyers. Tell family and friends, and ask them to spread the word.

When the day comes, a parent, a guardian, or another trusted adult can help you put out Free Car Wash signs that direct traffic to you. You might get a few stops, or you might have a line of cars waiting. Each vehicle should get a quick wash. Each driver should get a flyer that promotes your business, explains your services, lists your rates, and shows your contact information. You'll probably get a few tips, especially if you post a sign that says, Tips Accepted. But more than that, you might land a few long-term clients.

After the event, keep advertising. If you have a good strategy for letting people know about your business, you have a chance to do well. Across the United States, the car-washing industry brings in $5.8 billion per year. Some of that money could be yours!

GARAGE ORGANIZING

Does your family have a garage? Is it neat and tidy? If so, you're probably in the minority. Most people's garages range from disorganized to downright dirty. Plenty of homeowners would pay someone to take care of that problem. With a little time—and a lot of sweat—you could give them the garage of their dreams.

This business isn't just about cleaning. There's also a lot of lifting and moving. In fact, to get the job done right, you might need a partner—someone who does part of the work, helps with the heavy lifting, and, of course, gets paid for it. If you know someone who's reliable and willing to work as hard as you, consider making that person a partner in your business. You'll share the workload and the responsibilities fifty-fifty. You'll also split the money.

If you'd rather run your business alone, you can do that instead. This way, you'll handle the smaller jobs by yourself. When you get a bigger job with heavy objects to move, hire a friend or a relative to help you, as needed.

Working Wisdom: Paid Assistants

When you hire an assistant to help you with a job, look for someone hardworking and dependable. Explain the job and your expectations. Say how much time you think the job will take and how much you'll pay. (The assistant's share should be less than half of what you're getting paid.) If your first choice accepts the offer, you're ready to roll. If not, offer the job to someone else. And of course, you don't have to hire the same assistant for every job. Build up a list of reliable helpers with different skills. That way, you'll always have backup if your top pick falls through. After a job, pay your assistant promptly. And remember to say thank you for a job well done!

It's always best to practice before you dive right in. Among your relatives and friends, you should be able to find a few garages to organize. Bring work gloves, a push broom, a dustpan, a bucket for soapy water, and some old rags.

Before you start, ask the garage owners for instructions. Find out if they want their possessions reorganized in a certain way and if there's anything you shouldn't move. Then get to work. Sort through boxes, cabinets, and shelves. Label unmarked containers with permanent marker. Keep related items close together. For instance, put gardening supplies on one shelf. Or gather sports equipment in a certain corner. Make sure the most commonly used items are easy to see and access. If the garage owners have young children, place most objects—except for their toys—out of their reach.

Throw out or recycle empty containers or broken tools. And if you come across an item that looks like junk but you're not quite sure, get the owner's okay before throwing it in the trash.

Be on the lookout for hazardous materials. You might come across containers of oil, fuel, paint, pesticides, and other dangerous products. Make sure these containers stay tightly sealed. If you find something that isn't clearly labeled, bring it to the owners' attention. Pick a safe place, such as a high shelf, to store these products. If you find spills or leaks of any kind, alert the owners and wait to continue your work until the material has been cleaned up (not by you). The same rule of thumb applies to broken glass, weapons, and dead critters such as mice. Your job is to clean—not to put yourself at risk.

As you work, wipe down flat surfaces with wet rags. Do the same for dirty or dusty objects. Finally, sweep the garage floor.

When you finish, show the owners and see what they think. Make sure they know where to find everything in their transformed garage. Then ask them to be references for you.

Armed with experience and a few good references, share the news of your business with family and friends. Ask them to recommend potential customers. You can get in touch with possible clients by phone or e-mail. Or you can stop by their homes to introduce yourself and hand out business cards. Plan to clean garages belonging to people you know or who are recommended to you by people you trust.

Keep a record of your customers and of when you cleaned for them. Contact them every six months or so to see if they need your services again. Of course, if you clean each client's garage only twice a year, you're going to need plenty of customers to keep your business thriving. That means more advertising.

Get permission to hang flyers at local hardware stores or lumberyards. You may even want to advertise in the local newspaper. The garage sale section is a smart spot for that.

While you're at it, you may also want to offer services in garage sale setup. After all, you may find a lot of unwanted items in clients' garages. Why not help them clean, organize, display, and price those items to sell?

Set a goal for the number of garages you hope to clean per month. Work hard on advertising until you consistently reach that goal. When you get there, you can consider your business a success.

FRAGILE, HANDLE WITH CARE

TUTORING

If you do well in school and like to teach, tutoring is a prime job opportunity for you. Make a difference in a young child's life—and earn some pretty good money—by becoming a tutor. You'll work one-on-one with other students, helping them with subjects in which they're struggling.

Tutoring can be very rewarding. But it also takes the right kind of person. You must be patient, understanding, and focused yet flexible.

The good news is you don't need to be a super genius to tutor. You just need to be an expert at *something*. Maybe you're not so great at science but happen to be a grammar whiz. You might be cut out to tutor English. Or maybe you're struggling with geometry this year, but you aced last year's math classes. You can tutor younger kids in the material you've mastered.

You don't have to stick to the most obvious subjects, either. For instance, if you're a native Spanish speaker, you might be a great Spanish tutor. If you play the piano, perhaps you can offer lessons.

Bottom line: offer your services only in subjects that you know well. More important, you should tutor only in subjects that you truly enjoy.

Practice makes perfect, so start by volunteering. Ask around to see if any teachers can use your help before or after school. This could mean anything from tidying up their classrooms to preparing supplies for the next day. By being around teachers, you're bound to pick up some good teaching habits. Plus, the teachers you're helping now might refer students to you in the future.

While you're still learning, offer to tutor your relatives, classmates, friends—and their younger siblings. This will give you valuable teaching experience. It will also help you decide what subjects and what age levels are best suited to you. Plus, you can ask parents of your "practice students" to write you reference letters. Make copies of those letters and give them to people who are thinking about hiring you.

When you're ready for business, decide on your hourly rate. Then put the word out about your services. Tell everyone you know, and have your parents do the same. See if you can put flyers in school offices and teachers' lounges. You might even want to do a brief presentation at a PTA meeting.

When you get a client, meet with the parents. Find out why they're hiring you. What do they want for their child? What are their specific goals? Does the child have special needs? How often would the family like you to meet with the child? For how long? (Sessions normally last between thirty minutes and an hour.)

You may also want to meet with your client's teacher. The teacher may know more about why a student is struggling and have suggestions for how you can help. It's also helpful to get a clear idea of the teacher's expectations for a student. Once you know the overall goals for a client's tutoring sessions—and what the student's specific difficulties are—you can plan each session. Get familiar with the textbook or other learning materials that the student is using. Look ahead to find out what the next lessons will be. Or see if you can get a schedule from the teacher.

Find schoolwork and games that help to teach each lesson. Create a script, or a lesson plan, for how much time you'll spend on each activity. This lesson plan can come from your own ideas, from teachers, from other tutors, and from research. Many teaching websites—and sites devoted to a specific subject—have games, worksheets, and other resources you can use. But in many ways, you are your own best resource. You know this material. You enjoy it. You had to learn it once. Draw on the tools that were helpful to you.

Then tweak those tools to fit your client's learning style. Some students are visual learners. Some learn better by writing things down. As you get to know your clients, you'll find out what works best for each of them.

Working Wisdom: Setting Rates

Choosing an hourly rate for any business is tricky. You want to make as much money as you can. But the people who hire you want to pay as little as possible. You need to choose an amount that keeps you happy. And it has to be an amount your clients are willing to pay. Start low and raise your prices as you get busier—and as you gain a reputation for being worth the extra money.

You might meet at your client's home, at yours, at school, or at a local library. The setting should be comfortable, quiet, and free from distractions. At the beginning of each session, set a timer on your phone or watch so you can stick to your time limit. Some activities may take longer than you planned, but only extend the session if you have an employer's permission.

It's up to you to keep your client working. Your sessions together should be enjoyable for both of you. But no matter what, you need to make progress toward the goals. Keep in mind that you're there to *teach* the homework, not to *do* it. You might have to work through most or all the assignment with your client. But always ask yourself, "Is what I'm doing helping this student learn?" Encourage your clients to let you know when they don't understand something. Make it clear that it's okay if they get a wrong answer. And ask for feedback on your teaching strategies. If a client is bored by an activity or finds it hard to follow, you might want to try a different approach. But if a student clearly isn't making an effort, talk to his or her parents. You can't teach a client who isn't willing to try.

After each session, document what you did and note any progress. That way, you can show your employers the progress their child has made. They'll be impressed by how organized you are. And they'll be more likely to keep working with you for the weeks, months, and years to come.

TEACHING SOCIAL MEDIA

Are you good with computers? Do you like to teach? Are you active on social media? If that sounds like you, then you might be cut out for this up-and-coming job. More and more people want to start using social media sites, such as Facebook, Twitter, and Pinterest. But they don't know how. The right person could build a business teaching them.

You don't need to be a total expert in social media. Your clients probably aren't going to ask how to get ten thousand likes on Facebook. But you do need to know the basics, such as opening an account, connecting with friends, sending private messages, and uploading or downloading photos. You also need to be very patient and understanding. Some clients might not be very good at typing. Some might not even know how to use the Internet.

Practice with relatives. See if you can teach your parents, grandparents, or a younger sibling how to use social media. (But make sure you have adult permission to tutor anyone younger than you.) If they're new to the site or the skill you're explaining, this will

Working Wisdom: Stick to the Schedule

When you're running your own business, budgeting your time is as important as budgeting your money. Use a schedule book to keep track of when you're free to work. School should still be your first priority. So leave enough time for homework and extracurricular activities. Also mark family commitments in your scheduler—whether it's a weekly dinner with the grandparents or a once-a-year holiday gathering.

Before you take on a client, find out how much time the job will take. Will it be a few hours once a week? Half an hour once a month? Will it last for just a few sessions, a season, or longer? Only agree to jobs that fit in your schedule. Then make sure you always show up on time! If you have to cancel because of sickness, an emergency, or another unexpected conflict, contact your client as soon as possible, and offer to reschedule.

be a real test of your teaching talents. Even if they're already social media savvy, the experience of teaching is invaluable. Your "students" can give you pointers about your approach, and you'll learn what works and what doesn't. You'll also find out if you enjoy the job.

As for the topics you'll be offering, Internet and e-mail use are essential. If you're old enough to have accounts at social media sites such as Facebook and Twitter, you can include those on your menu of services. (Other possibilities include Pinterest, Google+, Instragram, and, of course, YouTube.) And the more you know about phones, the better. Many people know how to use social media on computers but need help to figure out how to do the same things on a mobile

device. If you can show clients how to make the transition, you'll be in high demand.

Practice each lesson at least a few times before launching your business. In this line of work, you could get a lot of word-of-mouth customers. That means your clients might tell other potential clients about you. So make sure that you do excellent work from the start.

You can expect many of your customers to be around your grandparents' age. Plan your advertising efforts with that in mind. Ask yourself, "Where in my area will senior citizens be?" That's where you want to promote your business. Get permission to hang up flyers at local cafés, grocery stores, health clinics, or dentist offices. Place an ad in a community newsletter or the local newspaper. Better yet, write a short "how-to" article related to social media. (Mention your business and contact information in that article.)

Is there a senior center or an adult living community nearby? Volunteer to do a thirty-minute presentation there. Teach something specific, such as how to open a Twitter account. Then leave at least ten minutes at the end to answer questions.

Let your family and friends promote you too. In particular, if you know any local grandparents, give them your business cards to pass out on your behalf.

Before accepting a client, ask what he or she expects to learn. That way, you'll both have a clear goal before the work begins. Also, find out what resources your client has. What kind of computer does your client use? Does he or she have a reliable Internet connection? If not, you might want to meet at your place or somewhere with free

Wi-Fi, such as a local café. (But only suggest this if your client has a laptop or other portable device to bring. Clients who only have desktops will need you to come to them.)

Choose your hourly rate. Then charge that much *per session*. Tell clients that each session will last "up to an hour." If the client masters a skill in twenty minutes, you can take your money and be on your way. If the client struggles, the frustration only grows after working longer than an hour. Stop there and give your client some simple steps to practice. Take your payment and schedule another session for a later date.

No matter how quickly or slowly your clients learn, if you are patient and respectful, the experience will be good for all involved.

PARTING WORDS

Putting money in your pocket feels pretty good. Knowing that you earned it by helping someone else feels even better. So are you ready to start your own business?

No matter which job you choose, success starts with practice. Get the skills and training you need. Then go out there and find clients. Stay focused on meeting your customers' needs, and you'll be earning money in no time!

NOW WHAT?

If you want to launch your business, begin with an action plan. To do that, grab a sheet of paper or hop onto a computer. Then answer these questions:

How much money will your business cost to start? How will you get that money? How will you pay it back?

Are there ongoing expenses after you begin? What are they? How will you manage your budget to pay for these expenses?

What are your goals? How many clients do you hope to have? How much do you hope to earn per hour? How much will you want to make per week or month?

Will you need to file a tax return? By federal law, you must file a tax return if you earn more than a certain amount of money per year. Have an adult help you check IRS Publication 929 to find out what to do.

What strategies will you use to find clients? Where and how will you advertise?

Will you work alone? Will you have a partner? Will you hire someone to help you? If so, list a few good candidates.

GLOSSARY

budget: an estimate of the amount of money you'll earn and the amount of money you'll need to pay for expenses. If you keep close track of your budget, you should have enough money for supplies.

business card: a small, rectangular card that lists your name, business, and how to contact you. Carry business cards with you, and hand them out to all potential clients.

contact information: phone numbers, e-mail addresses, and other ways to get in touch with someone

invest: to put money into a business with hopes of gaining even more money back. To start your new business, you might need to invest money into it.

nonprofit business: a business that spends all of its profits (if any) on improving its services. An animal shelter is an example of a nonprofit business.

profit: money gained after costs are subtracted from total earnings. Your total earnings from mowing a lawn minus the cost of the gas for your lawn mower will be your profit.

reference: a person who agrees to speak with potential employers about you and the work that you do. When you do volunteer work, ask a person you're volunteering for to be a reference.

FURTHER INFORMATION

Bernstein, Daryl. *Better Than a Lemonade Stand! Small Business Ideas for Kids.* New York: Aladdin, 2012. Discover several small business ideas for kids.

Donovan, Sandy. *Job Smarts: How to Find Work or Start a Business, Manage Earnings, and More.* Minneapolis: Twenty-First Century Books, 2012. Read about how to find and succeed in the right kind of job for you.

Harmon, Daniel E. *First Job Smarts.* New York: Rosen Publishing, 2010. Learn how to prepare yourself for starting your first job.

It's My Life: Making Money
http://pbskids.org/itsmylife/money/making/index.html
This PBS website offers tips for figuring out what jobs are good fits for you.

Orr, Tamra. *Money-Making Opportunities for Teens Who Like Working Outside.* New York: Rosen Publishing, 2014. This book from the Make Money Now! series focuses on jobs outdoors.

Teaching Kids Business
http://www.teachingkidsbusiness.com
Visit this page for a program that will help you prepare for your new business.

Youth & Labor
http://www.dol.gov/dol/topic/youthlabor
For the dos and don'ts of working before age 16, check out the Department of Labor's website.

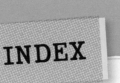

INDEX

adults: help from, 6–7, 23; permission from, 32
advertising, 8, 11, 15–16, 17–18, 20, 22–23, 27, 29, 34
assistants, 20, 24–25

babysitting, 13–16
business cards, 7, 8–9, 12, 18–19, 22, 26, 34

car washing, 20–23

dog walking, 17–19
door-knocking, 8, 11, 12, 17, 22

flyers, 22–23, 27, 29, 34

garage organizing, 24–27

lawn mowing, 6–9, 11

on call, 11–12

rates, 9, 12, 15, 18, 20, 23, 29, 30, 35
references, 7, 14, 26, 29

schedule, 9, 20, 33, 35
startup costs, 6–7, 11, 21
supplies, 6–7, 11, 16, 19, 21, 25, 34–35

teaching social media, 32–35
time limit, 31
tips, 23
training, 13–14, 35
tutoring, 28–31

volunteering, 7, 11, 14, 16, 17–18, 21, 25, 29, 32–34

yard services, 10–12

PHOTO ACKNOWLEDGMENTS

The images in this book are used with the permission of: © Alex ko/
Shutterstock.com, pp. 2, 4, 6, 8 (grass); © photka/Shutterstock.com,
pp. 2, 3, 6 , 7, 8, 9, 10, 12 (dandelion flowers); © iStockphoto.com/
disarrays, pp. 4, 5, 20, 22, 23, 27(sponge); © zirconicusso/Shutterstock.
com, p. 5 (rubber ducks); © HelenaQueen/Shutterstock.com, pp. 5
(dog); © Menna/Shutterstock.com, p. 10 (flowers); © iStockphoto.com/
najin, pp. 10, 11, 12 (leaf); © George Filyagin/Shutterstock.com, p. 13
(crayons); © iStockphoto.com/vicm, p. 13 (blocks); © Nenov Brothers
Images/Shutterstock.com, p. 14 (blocks); © Cheryl E. Davis/Shutterstock.
com, p. 16 (rattle); © Eric Isselee/Shutterstock.com, p. 18 (tennis ball);
© Fly_dragonfly/Shutterstock.com, p. 19 (dog); © iStockphoto.com/
FreeSoulProduction, p. 19 (paw and footprints); © pterwort/Shutterstock.
com, p. 21 (car wash sign); © Mike Flippo/Shutterstock.com, p. 21
(cleaning supplies); © nito/Shutterstock.com, p. 23 (squeegee); © Boris
Sosnovyy/Shutterstock.com, p. 23 (hose); © J. Helgason/Shutterstock.
com, pp. 24, 26, 27 (cardboard box); © Skylines/Shutterstock.com, p. 27
(cleaning supplies); © Karen Roach/Shutterstock.com, pp. 28, 29, 31
(colored pencils); © Art-Hunters/Shutterstock.com, p. 28 (colored pencil
shavings); © Voldymyr Krasyuk/Shutterstock.com, p. 29 (pens); © Cienpies
Design/Shutterstock.com, p. 32 (icons); © Nata-Lia/Shutterstock.com,
p. 34 (cable); © Roman Sotola/Shutterstock.com, pp. 34, 35 (cursor).

Front cover: © Javier Brosch/Shutterstock.com (dog); © Iakov Filimonov/
Shutterstock.com (lawn mower).

Main body text set in Avenir LT Std 11/18.
Typeface provided by Adobe Systems.